Connecticut

BY ANN HEINRICHS

Content Adviser: Dr. Jon Emmett Purmont, Professor of History, Southern Connecticut State University, West Haven, Connecticut

Reading Adviser: Dr. Linda D. Labbo, Department of Reading Education, College of Education, The University of Georgia

COMPASS POINT BOOKS MINNEAPOLIS, MINNESOTA

Compass Point Books
3109 West 50th Street, #115
Minneapolis, MN 55410

Visit Compass Point Books on the Internet at *www.compasspointbooks.com*
or e-mail your request to *custserv@compasspointbooks.com*

On the cover: Connecticut state capitol in Hartford

Photographs ©: Corbis/Alan Schein Photography, cover, 1; Audrey Gibson/The Image Finders, 3, 20;
Unicorn Stock Photos/Gary Randall, 5; Steve Callahan/Visuals Unlimited, 6; Corbis/Lee Snider, 7;
Photo Network, Patti McConville, 8, 25, 29 (bottom), 42, 47; Courtesy of AlpineZone.com, 9;
Unicorn Stock Photos/H. Schmeiser, 10, 41; Unicorn Stock Photo/Chuck Schmeiser, 12, 30; North
Wind Picture Archives, 13, 14, 15, 24, 28; Hulton/Archive by Getty Images, 16; Bettman/Corbis, 17;
Corbis, 18; Courtesy of Robert Caroti/Connecticut General Assembly, 22, 43 (top); Photo Network/TJ
Florian, 23; U.S. Department of Agriculture/Bill Tarpenning, 26; Corbis/Raymond Gehman, 27; Stock
Montage, 29 (top), 46; Leonard Friend, 31; Photo Courtesy of Loon Meadow Farm, Norfolk, CT, 32,
45; Bob Wilson/Visuals Unlimited, 33; Courtesy of The Maritime Aquarium at Norwalk/Jim Herity, 34,
48 (top); Corbis/Roman Soumar, 36; Mark E. Gibson/Visuals Unlimited, 37, 40; N. Carter/North Wind
Picture Archives, 38; Science VU/Visuals Unlimited, 39; Robesus, Inc., 43 (state flag); One Mile Up,
Inc., 43 (state seal); William J. Weber/Visuals Unlimited, 44 (top); Robert McCaw, 44 (middle);
Comstock, 44 (bottom).

Editors: E. Russell Primm, Emily J. Dolbear, and Patricia Stockland
Photo Researcher: Marcie C. Spence
Photo Selector: Linda S. Koutris
Designer: The Design Lab
Cartographer: XNR Productions, Inc.

Library of Congress Cataloging-in-Publication Data
Heinrichs, Ann.
  Connecticut / by Ann Heinrichs.
      p. cm.— (This land is your land)
Includes bibliographical references and index.
Contents: Welcome to Connecticut!—Hills, valleys, and coasts—A trip through time—Government
by the people—Connecticut at work—Getting to know Connecticut's people—Let's explore
Connecticut!
  ISBN 0-7565-0340-X
  1. Connecticut—Juvenile literature. [1. Connecticut.] I. Title. II. Series: Heinrichs, Ann. This land is
your land.
  F94.3 .H45 2003
  974.6—dc21   2002012864

Table of Contents

4 Welcome to Connecticut!

6 Hills, Valleys, and Coasts

13 A Trip Through Time

20 Government by the People

24 Connecticut at Work

28 Getting to Know Connecticut's People

33 Let's Explore Connecticut!

41 Important Dates

42 Glossary

42 Did You Know?

43 At a Glance

44 State Symbols

44 Making Banana-Nutmeg Shakes

45 State Song

46 Famous Connecticut People

47 Want to Know More?

48 Index

NOTE: In this book, words that are defined in the glossary are in **bold** *the first time they appear in the text.*

"The Foundation of Authority is laid firstly in the Free consent of the People." The Reverend Thomas Hooker spoke these words in 1638. He was preaching to people in the Connecticut **Colony.** At that time, Great Britain's king ruled the colonies. However, Hooker believed people should govern themselves.

The **colonists** listened to Hooker and agreed with him. The next year, Connecticut adopted its Fundamental Orders. It was the American colonies' first constitution, or basic set of laws. It gave citizens the right to elect their leaders. That same idea is found in the U.S. Constitution. Naturally, Connecticut's nickname is the Constitution State.

Connecticut quickly became a leading **industrial** state. Even in the 1700s, its factories made many useful goods. Connecticut's factories are still busy today. Some of their top products are **helicopters** and **submarines.** At the same time, Connecticut protects its beautiful **wilderness** areas. Visitors enjoy the state's natural beauty and many historic sites. Now come explore Connecticut. You're sure to enjoy it, too!

▲ Connecticut's natural beauty can be seen at Kent Falls State Park.

Connecticut is one of the six New England states. The others are Maine, Massachusetts, New Hampshire, Rhode Island, and Vermont. They're in the far northeastern corner of the country. Connecticut is a very small state. It could fit inside Texas fifty-three times! Only Delaware and Rhode Island are smaller than Connecticut.

North of Connecticut is Massachusetts. To the west is New York. Rhode Island lies to its east. Connecticut's

▲ An island off the coast of Connecticut in Long Island Sound

▲ The Housatonic River runs under a covered bridge in West Cornwall.

southern coast faces Long Island Sound. That's an arm of the Atlantic Ocean.

The Connecticut River runs down the center of the state. It's New England's longest river. Connecticut settlers built their first towns along this river. One settlement—Hartford— is now the state capital. The Housatonic and Naugatuck Rivers flow through western Connecticut. In the east are the Thames and Quinebaug Rivers. All their waters empty into Long Island Sound.

Highlands rise east and west of the river. The western highlands are rough and rocky. They include the Litchfield Hills and the Norfolk Hills. Rivers and streams cut deep valleys through the wooded hills. Kent Falls is the largest of the area's many waterfalls.

▲ The town of Greenfield Hill is bordered on the west by highlands.

▲ **Mount Bear is part of the Taconic Mountains landscape.**

New England's Taconic Mountains reach into northwest Connecticut. This is a wild and rugged region with dense forests. The state's highest point, Mount Frissell, rises there.

▲ **The Stamford Museum and Nature Center is a fun place to visit.**

The hills of eastern Connecticut are much lower. They, too, are forest-covered. The highlands gently slope down toward the coast. Beaches, bays, marshes, and rocky shores line Connecticut's coast. Bridgeport, New Haven, Stamford, and Norwalk became great seaport towns. Today, they're some of Connecticut's largest cities.

Forests cover more than half the state. Foxes, muskrats, and rabbits scurry through the woods. Grouse, pheasants, and partridges rustle around among the leaves. Along the shore are clams, oysters, and lobsters.

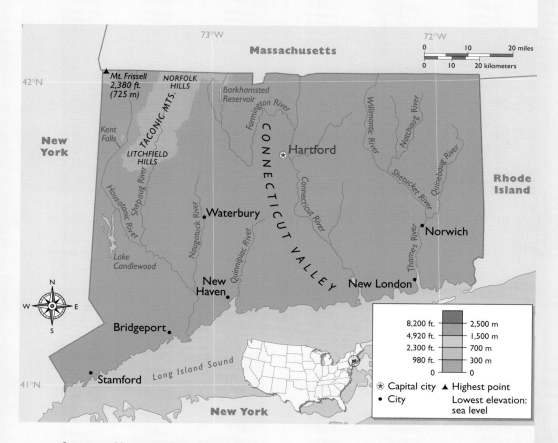

▲ **A topographic map of Connecticut**

▲ **Bright fall colors bring many visitors to Connecticut.**

Connecticut has hot summers and cold winters. The coast doesn't often get extremely cold or hot. The ocean waters act as a sort of shield. Summer is warmest on the southwestern coast. The northwest gets the coldest winters and the heaviest snows. Fall is a beautiful time of year in Connecticut. People come from far away to see the colorful leaves.

Before Europeans arrived, many Algonquian Indians lived in Connecticut. The Pequot people were the major group. They lived along Long Island Sound. Some Pequots split off and called themselves the Mohegan. They grew corn along the Thames River. They also caught fish. In the forests, they hunted wild animals. The animals provided meat and hides. The Nipmuc and Niantic were some of the neighboring groups.

▲ Algonquian Indians built lodges like this when they lived in Connecticut.

In the 1600s, Great Britain began setting up colonies. People from the Plymouth Colony moved into present-day Connecticut. They founded Windsor in 1633. This was Connecticut's first permanent European settlement. Soon, other colonists built the towns of Wethersfield and Hartford. These three towns became the Connecticut Colony in 1636. The set of laws they drew up was used as an example for the U.S. Constitution. Democracy was a main part of these laws.

Meanwhile, colonists and Native Americans began fighting the Pequot War (1637). Colonists attacked a Pequot fort

▲ **Pilgrims at the Plymouth settlement**

at Mystic in 1637. Hundreds of Pequot people were killed. In 1638, the Pequots were forced to leave.

Britain's King Charles II gave Connecticut a royal charter in 1662. That made it an official British colony. Soon, the town of New Haven was part of the colony. The next king, James II, wanted New England combined under one governor. In 1687, Governor Sir Edmund Andros marched his soldiers into Hartford. He demanded Connecticut's charter. Legend says the colonists hid their charter in an old oak tree. This tree, the Charter Oak, became Connecticut's state tree.

Soon, all the colonists were tired of Great Britain's taxes and laws. They fought for freedom in the Revolution-

▲ The story of hiding Connecticut's charter in the oak is an important part of the state's history.

▲ Jonathan Trumbull supported fighting in the Revolutionary War.

ary War (1775–1783). Even Connecticut's governor, Jonathan Trumbull, wanted freedom. He was the only colonial governor to support the war. Parts of Connecticut were heavily damaged during the war. On September 6, 1781, Benedict Arnold led British troops on an attack of New London. Most of the town's buildings were burned.

At last, the colonists won the war. They would form the new United States of America. First, however, each of the thirteen colonies had to approve the U.S. Constitution. It contained the nation's basic set of ideas and laws.

It wasn't easy for everyone to agree on a Constitution. However, Connecticut's leaders had experience with their Fundamental Orders. They were able to get everyone to agree on how many representatives each state would have in

Congress. This was called the Great Compromise. Connecticut became the fifth U.S. state in 1788.

Many factories opened in the 1800s. Mystic and other seaport towns were famous for shipbuilding. Eli Whitney taught people a lot about **mass-producing** goods. He made an object's parts in standard shapes and sizes. That made

▲ **Workers helping build a boat**

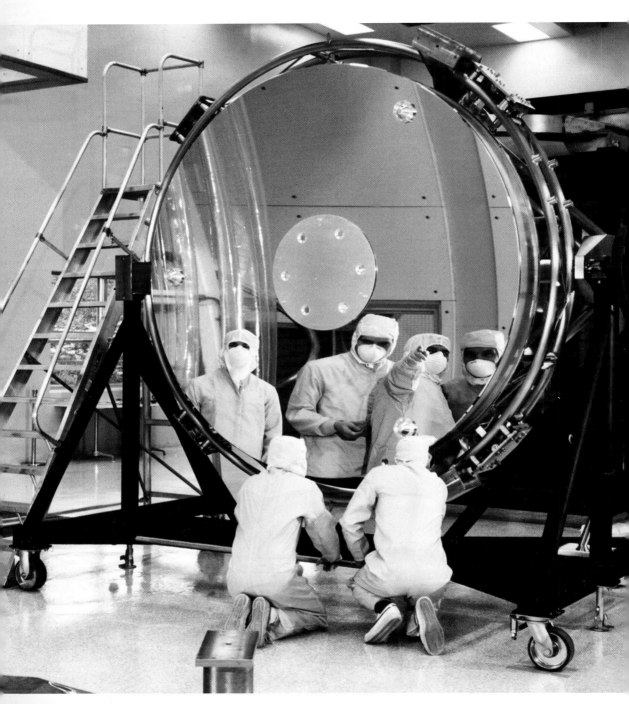

▲ This space telescope mirror for NASA was built in Wilton, Connecticut.

manufacturing much quicker and easier. Soon, Connecticut was a leading manufacturing state. Immigrants from many countries came to work in these factories.

Connecticut played an important role in defending the country. It helped in both World War I (1914–1918) and World War II (1939–1945). The state made submarines, guns, airplane parts, and other supplies. Connecticut even helped in space exploration. U.S. astronauts landed on the Moon in 1969. In their backpacks were many supplies from Connecticut.

Today, Connecticut is still an industrial leader. Its people have a high average **income.** The state works hard to keep its **environment** clean and safe. It also works to improve public schools and housing. State leaders have one goal—making Connecticut a great place to live.

▲ **The state capitol in Hartford**

The people of Connecticut are experts at government. Remember? This is the Constitution State.

Connecticut's state government today is much like the U.S. government. It's divided into three branches—legislative, executive, and judicial. These three branches make for a good balance. They spread the governing power around.

The legislative branch makes the state laws. It also decides how the state will spend its money.

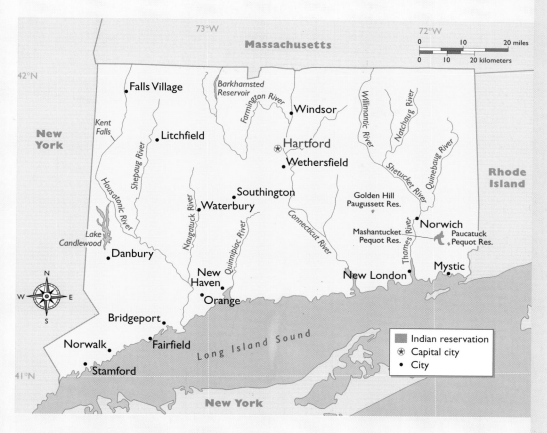

▲ A geopolitical map of Connecticut

Connecticut's lawmakers serve in the general assembly. It's composed of two houses, or sections. One is the 36-member senate. The other is the 151-member house of representatives. Voters elect their lawmakers from districts divided by population.

The executive branch enforces, or carries out, the laws. Connecticut's governor is the head of the executive branch.

▲ A legislative office building in Hartford

Voters choose a governor every four years. The governor can serve any number of terms. Voters also elect the lieutenant governor, attorney general, and other executive officers.

The judicial branch decides whether laws have been broken. This branch is made up of judges. They preside over courts. Connecticut's highest court is the state supreme court. It has seven justices, or judges.

Connecticut is divided into eight counties. However, there are no county governments. Rhode Island is the only other state organized this way. Instead, Connecticut's 169 towns handle local government. They elect a mayor or manager and a town council. A "town" might cover a large area with many communities. Larger towns have cities or boroughs within them. Many smaller towns are governed by town meetings. Their citizens meet every year and vote on important issues.

▲ The old town hall building in Norfolk dates back to 1840.

Connecticut at Work

In colonial times, "Yankee **peddlers**" wandered through Connecticut. They were salesmen who traveled from house to house. They sold housewares, tools, and all kinds of gadgets. Connecticut's factories produced much of their merchandise. Even in the 1700s, they made clocks, nails, and guns. Connecticut was also a leader in shipbuilding and steelmaking.

Today, Connecticut's major factory goods are machines. They include computers, engines, and office equipment. Other

▲ **A peddler selling merchandise out of his wagon**

Connecticut products travel by air and sea. They are airplane parts, helicopters, and submarines. Most are for military use. Small metal goods are important, too. Connecticut is known for its knives and other hardware. That includes tools, nuts, bolts, and metal pipes.

Before the Revolutionary War, Connecticut was a farming state. Today, most Connecticut farms are small. Farmers raise crops on about half the state's farmland. The other half is grazing land. The top farm products are decorative plants. They

▲ **A flower nursery in Litchfield**

include shrubs, flowers, and Christmas trees. Corn, hay, and tobacco are the major field crops. Apples are the state's major fruit. Some farmers grow grapes, too. Do you like mushrooms? Well, Connecticut produces a lot of them.

Chickens and eggs are important farm products. So are dairy products. Dairy farmers sell their milk to city markets. Other farmers raise beef cattle, sheep, and hogs. Connecticut's coastal waters yield a lot of shellfish. Lobsters and oysters bring in the most fishing income. Clams and scallops are

▲ Holstein cows produce milk, which is an important product for Connecticut.

▲ **Fishers catching oysters in Long Island Sound**

important catches, too. Fishing boats also bring in bluefish, bass, flounder, and shad.

Crushed stone, sand, and gravel are Connecticut's leading minerals. They're mostly used to make concrete and to build roads.

Service industries are very important to Connecticut. Insurance, moneylending, and real estate are the top services. Hartford is called the insurance capital of the world! Service workers hold jobs in many other areas. They may be teachers, health care workers, or store clerks. They may drive trucks, sell cars, or fix bikes. They all use their skills to help others.

▲ Samuel Clemens (Mark Twain) was an important American writer.

Remember those Yankee peddlers? Some people believed the peddlers were a bit tricky. They said peddlers pretended to sell the spice **nutmeg,** yet they were really selling nut-shaped pieces of wood. This old tale earned Connecticut's people the nickname Nutmeggers. However, this is not an insult. It means Nutmeggers are good at inventing things!

Author Mark Twain used this idea in one of his books. It's called *A Connecticut Yankee in King Arthur's Court.* The hero traveled back to the year 538. He missed all the comforts of the 1800s, so he got busy. He invented ways to make soap, telephones, and other handy items.

Twain lived in Hartford for many years. There he wrote *The Adventures of Tom Sawyer* and other popular books. He's just one of Connecticut's famous writers. Another is Harriet Beecher Stowe. Her book *Uncle Tom's Cabin* shows the horrors of slavery.

How is your spelling? Pretty good? So-so? Noah Webster's spelling was awesome! He published America's first dictionary. Webster went to Yale University in New Haven. Founded in 1701, Yale is America's third-oldest college.

▲ Harriet Beecher Stowe wrote a book that spoke out against slavery.

▲ Yale University is located in New Haven.

▲ The entrance to "Holy Land, U.S.A.," a tourist attraction and shrine near Waterbury

Nutmeggers are packed tightly into their small state. In 2000, there were 3,405,565 people in Connecticut. Only three other states have more people per square mile. Bridgeport is Connecticut's largest city, and New Haven is second. Next in size are Hartford, Stamford, and Waterbury.

Connecticut's early settlers had roots in England. Many immigrants arrived in the late 1800s and early 1900s. They came from Ireland, Italy, Germany, Russia, and many other nations. Many of their descendants still live in Connecticut. About one out of eleven residents is African-American. Most live in the big cities. Another one out of eleven people is

Hispanic. Some Asian and Native American people live in Connecticut, too.

Basketball is big in Connecticut. The men's and women's teams from the University of Connecticut are some of the best in the country. In 2003, the Connecticut Sun of the Women's National Basketball Association (WNBA) began playing in the state. There are many other fun activities, too. Southington holds an Apple Harvest Festival in September. Other towns hold country fairs in the fall. Mystic holds a big Lobsterfest in

▲ **Dogwood Festival in Fairfield**

▲ A couple enjoys a horse-drawn sleigh ride through the snow.

May. Meanwhile, the Dogwood Festival draws crowds to Fairfield in the spring. The dogwood trees are in bloom all over town then.

People bundle up for their winter fun. Some head for the snowy hillsides to ski. Others enjoy old-fashioned sleigh rides through the woods.

What was life like in a seaport town? You'll see for yourself at Mystic Seaport. It was rebuilt to look like a whaling village of the 1800s. You'll see where sails, ropes, and other sailing gear were made. Are you curious about life for schoolchildren there? Just visit the schoolhouse. It has old desks, a

▲ **Mystic Seaport is designed to look like an 1800s whaling village.**

woodstove, and a blackboard. A famous pizza parlor is in Mystic, too. The movie *Mystic Pizza* put the town on the map.

You'll discover a different side of sea life in Norwalk. Its Maritime Aquarium features sea animals of Long Island Sound. Peek into the massive tanks. You'll see sharks, sea horses, seals, jellyfish, and several other creatures. Do you want a real hands-on experience? Reach into the Touch Tank. You'll handle live sea stars and crabs.

Bridgeport's Discovery Museum has a planetarium with exciting sky shows. You'll also explore the math and science of basketball there. The USS *Nautilus* Memorial is in Groton. You

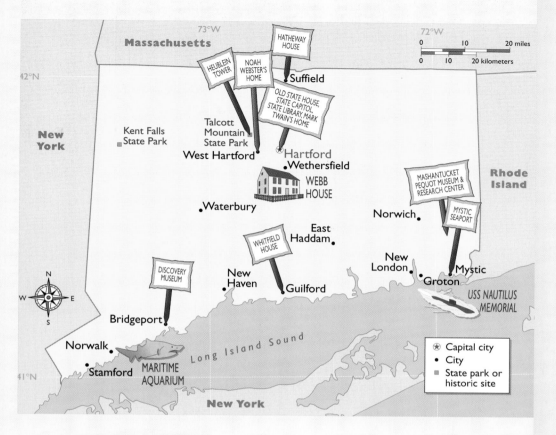

▲ **Places to visit in Connecticut**

can sit inside a submarine control room. You can also peer through a real periscope.

The Pequot people have a long history in Connecticut. Today, their museum in Mashantucket brings Pequot culture to life. The highlight is a life-sized Pequot village of the 1500s. There you can see how the Pequot built wigwams and made arrows.

▲ The Henry Whitfield House in Guilford is the oldest house in Connecticut.

In West Hartford, you can tour Noah Webster's home. There you can join in activities such as linen making. Many other buildings remain from colonial days. One is the Henry Whitfield House in Guilford. This old stone home is Connecticut's oldest house. It was built in 1639.

Webb House in Wethersfield is another historic site. General George Washington met with colonists there during the Revolutionary War. They planned the 1781 battle of Yorktown, Virginia. That battle ended the war. You can tour this home and two others nearby.

▲ **Webb House played an important role in the Revolutionary War.**

▲ **Nathan Hale was a talented teacher and a famous war hero.**

Nathan Hale taught school in both East Haddam and New London in the 1700s. Students from ages six through eighteen all studied in one room. "He was a happy and faithful teacher; everybody loved him," said a student. Hale went on to become a great Revolutionary War hero. Today, you can tour his two schoolhouses.

Hartford's Old State House was built in 1796. That's where the colony's early lawmakers met. You can watch today's lawmakers in the state capitol. At the state library, you'll see the colony's Fundamental Orders. You'll also see the colony's original 1662 charter. Its frame is made of wood from the Charter Oak.

You can visit Mark Twain's home in Hartford, too. You'll see the very same furniture he used every day. In Suffield, you can see the Phelps Homestead, now known as the Hatheway House. Its tavern, inn, and meeting house have been turned into a museum.

▲ The Victorian house in Hartford where Mark Twain lived

▲ **From Heublein Tower in Talcott Mountain State Park, you can see this beautiful countryside in Farmington Valley.**

History isn't the only thing that comes to life in Connecticut. You'll also want to enjoy its natural beauty. The forest-covered hills are great places for hiking. Climbing up to Heublein Tower is worth the effort. It's in Talcott Mountain State Park.

Gaze out from the tower on a clear day. You'll see four states—Connecticut, Massachusetts, New York, and Rhode Island. From here you can take in all the history and beauty that Connecticut has to offer. You'll agree that the Constitution State is great!

Important Dates

1614   Adriaen Block claims Connecticut for the Netherlands.

1633   Colonists make Connecticut's first settlement in Windsor.

1636   Hartford, Wethersfield, and Windsor settlers form the Connecticut Colony.

1638   New Haven is founded.

1639   Connecticut adopts the Fundamental Orders as its law.

1662   King Charles II grants the Connecticut Colony a charter.

1731   Border dispute between New York and Connecticut is settled.

1776   Captain Nathan Hale is hanged by the British for spying.

1788   Connecticut becomes the fifth U.S. state on January 9.

1833   Prudence Crandall opens New England's first academy for African-American women.

1910   The U.S. Coast Guard Academy moves to New London.

1954   The nuclear submarine *Nautilus* is launched in Groton.

1974   Ella Grasso is the first woman elected governor of Connecticut.

1990   Eunice S. Groark is the first woman elected lieutenant governor of Connecticut.

1999   The Hardford Courant wins the Pulitzer Prize for breaking news reporting; it was its second Pulitzer.

Glossary

colonists—people who settle a new land for their home country

colony—a territory that belongs to the country that settles it

environment—the air, water, trees, and other natural surroundings

helicopters—aircraft that can take off and land straight up and down

Hispanics—people of Mexican, South American, and other Spanish-speaking cultures

income—money regularly gained from working

industrial—having to do with a type of business or manufacturing

mass-producing—making products in large quantities by using machines and dividing work into simpler tasks to be done by people

nutmeg—a spice used in pumpkin pie and other desserts

peddlers—salespeople who travel from place to place

submarines—ships that travel underwater

wilderness—a wild, natural area

Did You Know?

★ The name *Connecticut* comes from a Mohegan Indian word. It means "long river place" or "beside the long tidal river."

★ Connecticut's famous Charter Oak blew down in a great storm in 1856.

★ The USS *Nautilus* put to sea from Groton in 1954. It was the world's first nuclear-powered submarine. It was also the first submarine to reach the North Pole.

★ New Haven issued the world's first telephone book in 1878. It listed only fifty names!

★ The *Hartford Courant* is the country's oldest newspaper that's still being published. It was established in 1764.

★ Noah Webster published his first dictionary in 1806. It's the ancestor of today's *Merriam-Webster Dictionary.*

★ Pez candy is made in Orange, Connecticut.

★ Stamford is the headquarters of World Wrestling Entertainment (WWE).

★ The *Charles W. Morgan* is in Mystic Seaport's harbor. It was New England's last wooden whaling ship.

State capital: Hartford

State motto: *Qui Transtulit Sustinet* (Latin for "he who transplanted still sustains")

State nickname: The Constitution State

Statehood: January 9, 1788; fifth state

Land area: 4,845 square miles (12,549 sq km); **rank:** forty-eighth

Highest point: South slope of Mount Frissell, 2,380 feet (725 m)

Lowest point: Sea level, along Long Island Sound

Highest recorded temperature: 106°F (41°C) at Danbury on July 15, 1995

Lowest recorded temperature: −32°F (−36°C) at Falls Village on February 16, 1943

Average January temperature: 26°F (−3°C)

Average July temperature: 71°F (22°C)

Population in 2000: 3,405,565; **rank:** twenty-ninth

Largest cities in 2000: Bridgeport (139,529), New Haven (123,626), Hartford (121,578), Stamford (117,083)

Factory products: Machines, transportation equipment, metal goods, scientific instruments

Farm products: Home and garden plants, milk, chickens, eggs

Mining products: Crushed stone, sand, gravel

State flag: Connecticut's state flag shows a shield with three grapevines. They stand for Connecticut's early colonists. Like transplanted vines, they "transplanted" themselves to their new home. Beneath them is a banner with the state motto, *Qui Transtulit Sustinet*. It's Latin for, "he who transplanted still sustains." The shield and banner are gold-edged white against a field of blue.

State seal: The state seal also shows three grapevines and the state motto.

State abbreviations: Conn. (traditional); CT (postal)

State Symbols

State bird: American robin

State flower: Mountain laurel

State tree: Charter oak

State animal: Sperm whale

State insect: European mantis

State shellfish: Eastern oyster

State mineral: Garnet

State fossil: *Eubrontes giganteus*

State ship: USS *Nautilus*

State hero: Nathan Hale

State heroine: Prudence Crandall

State composer: Charles Ives

State folk dance: Square dance

State commemorative quarter:
Released on October 12, 1999

Making Banana-Nutmeg Shakes

A delicious "Nutmegger" snack.

Makes four servings.

INGREDIENTS:

2 ripe bananas

1 $\frac{1}{2}$ cups milk

1 $\frac{1}{2}$ cups vanilla ice cream

2 tablespoons honey

$\frac{1}{2}$ teaspoon grated nutmeg

$\frac{1}{2}$ cup granola or nuts

DIRECTIONS:

Slice the bananas. Put them in a blender along with the other ingredients except the granola or nuts. Blend until smooth. Pour into glasses and sprinkle granola or nuts on top.

State Song

"Yankee Doodle"
Traditional words and music

Yankee Doodle went to town,
Riding on a pony,
Stuck a feather in his hat,
And called it macaroni.

Chorus:
Yankee Doodle keep it up,
Yankee Doodle dandy.
Mind the music and the step,
And with the folks be handy.

John Brown (1800–1859) fought to abolish slavery. He was executed after leading a raid on the U.S. Arsenal in Harpers Ferry, Virginia.

Thomas Gallaudet (1787–1851) opened America's first free school for the deaf in Hartford. Gallaudet University in Washington, D.C., a university for the deaf and hard of hearing, is named after him.

Charles Goodyear (1800–1860) invented the vulcanization process. It keeps rubber from sticking and melting in hot weather.

Nathan Hale (1755–1776) was a spy for the colonial forces in the Revolutionary War. The British captured and hanged him. His famous last words were, "I only regret that I have but one life to lose for my country."

Katharine Hepburn (1907–) is an actress who has won four Academy Awards. Her movies include *The Lion in Winter* and *On Golden Pond*.

Charles Ives (1874–1954) was a composer. His works are very original. He won the Pulitzer Prize for his Symphony no. 3.

John Pierpont Morgan (1837–1913) was a wealthy businessman. He helped start U.S. Steel, General Electric, and many other companies. He donated millions of dollars to charity and the arts.

Ralph Nader (1934–) is an activist for consumers' rights. He has fought for safe cars, safe meat, and many other causes.

Eugene O'Neill (1888–1953) wrote plays. Most of them have a dark message. Among his best-known plays are *The Iceman Cometh* and *A Long Day's Journey into Night.* He was born in New York City. As a young man, he attended school in Connecticut.

Harriet Beecher Stowe (1811–1896) worked to abolish slavery. Stowe (pictured above left) wrote the antislavery novel *Uncle Tom's Cabin.*

Mark Twain (1835–1910) is one of America's best-loved authors. He wrote *The Adventures of Tom Sawyer* while living in Hartford. He was born in Missouri as Samuel Clemens.

Noah Webster (1758–1843) compiled *An American Dictionary of the English Language* in 1828. It has been revised many times.

Eli Whitney (1765–1825) invented the cotton gin. It separates the cotton seeds from the fibers. His factories for cotton gins and muskets, or guns, were in New Haven. Whitney was born in Massachusetts.

Want to Know More?

At the Library

DePaola, Tomie. *26 Fairmount Avenue.* New York: Putnam Juvenile, 1999.

Curtis, Alice Turner, and Wuanita Smith (illustrator). *A Little Maid of Old Connecticut.* Bedford, Mass.: Applewood Books, 1997.

Furstinger, Nancy. *Connecticut.* Danbury, Conn.: Children's Press, 2002.

Lassieur, Allison. *The Pequot Tribe.* Mankato, Minn.: Bridgestone Books, 2001.

Murphy, Jim. *A Young Patriot: The American Revolution As Experienced by One Boy.* New York: Clarion Books, 1996.

Thompson, Kathleen. *Connecticut.* Austin, Tex.: Raintree/Steck-Vaughn, 1996.

Welsbacher, Anne. *Connecticut.* Edina, Minn.: Abdo & Daughters, 1998.

Whitehurst, Susan. *The Colony of Connecticut.* New York.: PowerKids Press, 2000.

On the Web

State of Connecticut

http://www.state.ct.us/
To learn about Connecticut's history, government, economy, and land

Connecticut Bound

http://www.tourism.state.ct.us/
To find out about Connecticut's events, activities, and sights

Through the Mail

Connecticut Office of Tourism

Department of Economic and Community Development
505 Hudson Street
Hartford, CT 06106
For information on travel and interesting sights in Connecticut

Connecticut Historical Society

One Elizabeth Street at Asylum Avenue
Hartford, CT 06105
For information on Connecticut's history

Connecticut Secretary of State

30 Trinity Street
Hartford, CT 06106
For information on Connecticut's state government

On the Road

Connecticut State Capitol

210 Capitol Avenue
Hartford, CT 06106
860/240-0222
To visit Connecticut's state capitol

Index

Adventures of Tom Sawyer, The (Mark Twain), 29
Algonquian Indians, 13
Andros, Sir Edmund, 15
animal life, 11, 26–27, 34
Apple Harvest Festival, 31
Arnold, Benedict, 16

borders, 6–7
Bridgeport, 11, 30, 34

Charles II, King of England, 15
Charter Oak, 15, 39
climate, 12
coastline, 11, 26–27
colonies, 4, 14, 15, 16
colonists, 4, 15, 16, 37
Connecticut Colony, 4, 14
Connecticut River, 7
Connecticut Sun (basketball team), 31
Connecticut Yankee in King Arthur's Court, A (Mark Twain), 28–29
Constitution of the United States, 4, 14, 16

Discovery Museum, 34–35
Dogwood Festival, 32

eastern highlands, 10
ethnic groups, 30–31
executive branch of government, 20, 21–22

Fairfield, 32
farming, 25–26

Fundamental Orders, 4, 16, 38

Great Compromise, 17
Guilford, 36

Hale, Nathan, 38
Hartford, 7, 14, 30, 36, 38, 39
Hatheway House, 39–40
Henry Whitfield House, 36
Heublein Tower, 40
highland region, 8, 10
Hooker, Thomas, 4
Housatonic River, 7

immigration, 19, 30

James II, King of England, 15
judicial branch of government, 20, 22

Kent Falls, 8

legislative branch of government, 20–21
Litchfield Hills, 8
Lobsterfest, 31
local government, 23. *See also* state government.
Long Island Sound, 7, 34

manufacturing, 4, 17, 19, 24–25
marine life, 26–27, 34
Maritime Aquarium, 34
mass-production, 17, 19

mining, 27
Mohegan tribe, 13
Mount Frissell, 9
Mystic, 15, 17, 31
Mystic Pizza (film), 34
Mystic Seaport, 33–34

Native Americans, 13, 14–15, 31, 35
Naugatuck River, 7
New Haven, 11, 15, 29, 30
New London, 16, 38
Norfolk Hills, 8
Norwalk, 11, 34

Old State House, 38

Pequot tribe, 13, 14–15, 35
Pequot War, 14–15
Phelps Homestead, 39
Plymouth Colony, 14
population, 30

Quinebaug River, 7

Revolutionary War, 15–16, 37, 38
rivers, 7, 13

service industries, 27
size, 6
sports, 31
Stamford, 11, 30
state capital, 7, 14, 30, 36, 38, 39
state capitol, 38

state government, 20–22. *See also* local government.
state nickname, 4
state tree, 15
statehood, 17
Stowe, Harriet Beecher, 29
Suffield, 39

Taconic Mountains, 9
Talcott Mountain State Park, 40
Thames River, 7, 13
Trumbull, Jonathan, 16
Twain, Mark, 28–29, 39

Uncle Tom's Cabin (Harriet Beecher Stowe), 29
USS *Nautilus* Memorial, 35

Washington, George, 37
Waterbury, 30
waterfalls, 8, 40
Webb House, 37
Webster, Noah, 29, 36
western highlands, 8
Wethersfield, 14, 37
Whitney, Eli, 17, 19
Windsor, 14
Women's National Basketball Association (WNBA), 31
World War I, 19
World War II, 19

Yale University, 29
"Yankee peddlers," 24, 28

About the Author

Ann Heinrichs grew up in Fort Smith, Arkansas, and lives in Chicago. She is the author of more than one hundred books for children and young adults on Asian, African, and U.S. history and culture. Ann has also written numerous newspaper, magazine, and encyclopedia articles. She is an award-winning martial artist, specializing in t'ai chi empty-hand and sword forms.

Ann has traveled widely throughout the United States, Africa, Asia, and the Middle East. In exploring each state for this series, she rediscovered the people, history, and resources that make this a great land, as well as the concerns we share with people around the world.